NATIONAL GEOGRAPHIC

Ladders

T0080582

BIG BEND
National Park

GENRE Social Studies Article

Read to find out how and why Big Bend National Park was created and preserved.

Strap on your backpack, find your sunglasses, and begin exploring Big Bend National Park. This park has many different types of landforms, including mountains, canyons, and deserts. What forces shaped this rugged land? Over hundreds of millions of years, oceans, earthquakes, and volcanoes formed and exposed the park's rocks. Wind and water then carved the peaks, canyons, and deserts we see here today.

WELCOME TO BIG BEND

by Cynthia Clampitt

Big Bend lies in the Chihuahuan (chih-WAH-wahn) Desert in southwestern Texas. In fact, Big Bend is named for the sharp turn, or "big bend," a river called the Rio Grande takes as it flows between the United States and Mexico. Most people think of deserts as hot places where few plants and animals can live, but that's not true of Big Bend. It can be hot, but Big Bend protects several unique desert **habitats**. It is one of the best places in the United States to see desert wildlife. In fact, this land has been full of living things since long before dinosaurs roamed here.

Big Bend's mountains are a challenge for climbers.

A TREASURED
NATIONAL PARK

The first people to live in this area were Native Americans who came about 10,000 years ago. Thousands of years later, the Spanish came looking for gold and other riches. Miners came searching for minerals, too. They didn't find gold, but they did find rocks that contained the metals silver and mercury.

The real treasures of Big Bend are its beautiful landforms and plentiful wildlife. To preserve them, Texas set aside this area as Texas Canyons State Park in the 1930s. In 1944, the park became a national park. It was renamed Big Bend. To help protect and preserve this fragile **ecosystem** even more, Big Bend is also a biosphere reserve.

> Big Bend bluebonnets bloom on the banks of the Rio Grande.

A **biosphere** is the combination of earth, air, and water that supports life. A reserve is a place for study. The Chihuahuan Desert is a biosphere with wildlife and special landforms. Big Bend was named a biosphere reserve in 1976.

Big Bend's biosphere has more than just living creatures. Some of its most famous creatures have been dead for millions of years! Thousands of **fossils** have been found here, including fossils of gigantic crocodiles and pterosaurs (TAIR-uh-sawrz), or flying reptiles. Researchers have found fossils of more than 90 types of dinosaurs at Big Bend. One find was of an enormous creature called Alamosaurus (AL-uh-moh-SAWR-uhs).

THE MAKING OF BIG BEND

1903
Cipriáno Hernandez builds a farm and store near the Rio Grande. The area grows into the town of Castolon.

1944

Big Bend becomes a national park to preserve and protect its unique landforms and wildlife.

1964
NASA's Apollo astronauts visit the park. They study volcanic rocks as they prepare to go to the moon.

1971
A college student finds fossil pterosaurs, or flying reptiles. They are some of the largest ever found.

2011

About 360,000 people visit Big Bend to hike, bike, canoe on the Rio Grande, and enjoy the wildlife.

THE WILDLIFE OF BIG BEND

Today, Big Bend is home to all types of living things. Flitting hummingbirds, swift roadrunners, soaring eagles, and many more kinds of birds live here. The park is home to more than 450 different species. But the bugs beat out the birds. Over 3,600 kinds of insects can be found in Big Bend. It's a bug paradise! All of these animals have adapted, or changed, to live in the Chihuahuan Desert.

JAVELINA

The javelina (hah-vuh-LEE-nuh) isn't a pig, but it sure looks like one. In Big Bend, javelinas usually travel in herds of about 14 animals. Other mammals in the park include mountain lions, black bears, bobcats, and coyotes.

How can this park support all this life? Big Bend has mountains as well as flat desert lands. Big Bend's mountains are cooler than its deserts. They get twice as much rain as its desert lands. This creates many habitats where certain plants and animals can live and grow. Let's look at a few of the creatures in Big Bend.

TARANTULA

A tarantula is one big spider. Some Big Bend tarantulas grow to be larger than the palm of your hand.

COLLARED LIZARD

This collared lizard can grow to be more than a foot long, and it can run on its hind legs.

LUBBER GRASSHOPPER

The lubber is a giant grasshopper. It can grow to be three inches long. This insect's bright colors warn animals not to eat it. It's poisonous.

Check In   What makes Big Bend different from other national parks?

GENRE Geography Tour

Read to find out about the birds of Big Bend National Park.

Welcome to Big Bend, bird-watchers! You've made it this far, so you know that this park is in a **remote** area of western Texas. It's so far from cities and towns that it's one of the least-visited national parks in the country. With so few crowds, the birds feel safe to fly around the park. In fact, Big Bend has more birds than any other national park.

Let's visit three different habitats, places where animals and plants live naturally. First, we'll see the birds of the Chisos Basin, high up in the mountains near the center of the park. Then we'll hike across the desert to the Chimneys, where birds nest near rock towers. We'll end on the banks of the Rio Grande, where the river has carved deep Santa Elena Canyon.

Birds aren't the only creatures that flock to Big Bend. Scientists flock here, too, in order to learn about Earth's history. Hundreds of millions of years of volcanoes, erosion, and earthquakes have pushed up and worn down the land in the park. This made the canyons, deserts, and rock formations that are homes for the park's 450 bird species. Grab your binoculars so we can check out the birds of Big Bend!

THE BIRDS OF BIG B[

by Cynthia Clampitt

BIG BEND'S BIRDING TOUR

Legend:

- – – – Route of Tour
- ――― Main Road
- ⊞⊞⊞ Dirt Road
- ――― 4-Wheel Drive only
- ‥‥‥ Hiking Trail
- ▬▬▬ Park Boundary

0   4   8 Miles
0   4   8 Kilometers

Park Entrance

1 Chisos Basin

LOST MINE TRAIL

2 The Chimneys

CHIMNEYS TRAIL

3 Santa Elena Canyon

TEXAS (U.S.)

MEXICO

Rio Grande

Big Bend National Park has beautiful deserts and high, rocky mountains.

① Chisos Basin: Mountain Birds

Our first stop is Chisos Basin. A **basin** is a low area drained by a river, but this basin is high in the Chisos Mountains. It's just lower than the peaks around it.

Let's hike the short Window View Loop Trail. The Window is a high canyon at the edge of the basin. Water flows from the mountains through the Window into the Chihuahuan Desert. Then it flows to the Rio Grande. Watch for birds along the trail. There are plenty up here, but it may be hard to see some of them.

The mountains are cooler than the desert below, so they attract many different types of birds that nest in the trees that grow up here. This is a good habitat for all kinds of birds, from tiny hummingbirds to large **raptors**, which are birds of prey, such as eagles.

If you hear noisy chattering, you'll know that an angry blue Mexican jay is scolding us for coming too close. If you're very patient and quiet, you might see a colorful Lucifer hummingbird sipping from the flower of a desert plant. Don't forget to look up because you may see a golden eagle!

Be sure to check out the bird photos on the right to see any you may have missed.

Λ Lucifer hummingbirds build their nests on steep, rocky slopes, such as those in the Chisos Mountains.

Λ As you can guess, most Mexican jays live in Mexico. However, many of these noisy blue birds also live in Big Bend National Park.

Λ Golden eagles can dive through the sky at speeds of more than 150 miles per hour to catch their prey.

∧ Roadrunners would rather scurry along the floor of the desert than fly above it. They can run more than 18 miles per hour.

∧ The cactus wren nests in cactus plants and gets its water from the food it eats. It has adapted well to desert living.

∧ The canyon towhee is a camouflage artist. Its brown and rusty feathers blend in with the desert floor to hide it from predators.

② The Chimneys: Desert Birds

Next, we'll hike through the desert to the Chimneys. Keep a close watch for desert birds along the way. The Chimneys Trail leads straight to those tall rock towers in the distance. It's flat and hot, with no shade, so put on your hat and sunblock, and let's go. Look! There's a roadrunner racing along the trail ahead of us. Roadrunners don't fly very well, so they usually hunt for snakes and lizards on the run.

As we hike, look for the cactus wren. It builds its nest in cactus plants and gets all its water from the insects and spiders it eats. That's good because it won't find many other water sources out here.

Listen. Do you hear that cheerful chirping that sounds like "chili, chili, chili"? That's a canyon towhee. These brown birds are easier to hear than to see because they blend in with their surroundings.

As we get nearer to the Chimneys, you might be wondering what they are doing out here in the middle of the desert. They formed when volcanoes erupted here long ago. Melted rock pushed up through cracks in Earth's crust and hardened to form sections of volcanic stone. When the softer rock around them wore away, the volcanic stone still stood like towers or chimneys.

③ The Rio Grande: River Birds

Our last stop is the Rio Grande, the river that forms part of the border between the United States and Mexico. To get a good look at river birds, we'll take canoes into Santa Elena Canyon. It has the park's tallest cliffs, which soar as high as 1,500 feet straight up. That's as tall as five football fields stacked end to end!

As we pass through the trees, look for holes in the bark. You might see the eyes of a tiny elf owl looking at you. These owls find holes in trees and cactus plants where they make their nests. They fly at night to hunt insects and spiders near the river.

Now that we're on the river, watch for great blue herons in the shallow water. The Rio Grande is a perfect habitat for these tall birds. They keep very still as they search for fish, frogs, lizards, and small mammals to eat.

Those flashes of red high on the cliffs are vermilion flycatchers hunting insects as they fly. They nest in the trees along the riverbanks and on top of canyon walls.

The sun is setting over Big Bend, and our day of bird-watching is over. We saw lots of different birds, but there are hundreds more to see here. Come back anytime, and bring your binoculars!

∧ Only male vermilion flycatchers are red. Females are brown. The males like to show off for the females by bringing them colorful butterflies to eat.

∧ Ever heard a bird that sounds like a dog? Meet the elf owl, which sounds like a poodle yapping. While unusual, its calls are a common sound during nights in Big Bend.

∧ The great blue heron is a wading bird, which is why it has such long legs. It is the largest wading bird in North America. It can grow to be four-and-a-half feet tall.

Check In | How are the birds of Big Bend suited to live in their different habitats?

In Search of the
LOST MINE

by Elizabeth Massie — Illustrated by Jan Lieffering

THE LOST MINE TRAIL, A FAMOUS HIKING TRAIL THAT BEGINS NEAR THE CENTER OF THE PARK, CLIMBS HIGH INTO BIG BEND'S CHISOS MOUNTAINS. IT'S NOT A LONG TRAIL, ONLY ABOUT FIVE MILES UP AND BACK, BUT PARTS OF IT ARE STEEP AND QUITE RUGGED. THE TRAIL IS NAMED AFTER A LEGENDARY MINE FULL OF GOLD. IS THERE REALLY A LOST GOLD MINE IN THE CHISOS, OR IS IT JUST A LEGEND? IF THIS MINE ACTUALLY DOES EXIST, WHERE MIGHT IT BE, AND WHAT ARE THE ODDS THAT SOMEONE MIGHT FIND IT ONE DAY?

Early one fall morning, the Jordan family put on their hiking boots, filled their water bottles, and started their trek. Mom, Dad, eleven-year-old Paul, and seven-year-old Angela were staying in Big Bend National Park, and they had been looking forward to a long hike in the mountains. Paul had read about the "Lost Mine Trail" in the park brochure, and the whole family wanted to explore it.

As they hiked into the Chisos Mountains, the family had fun identifying all the different lizards, birds, and plants. Paul pointed to a bristly tree and checked his brochure again. "That's called an alligator juniper. Its bark is scaly, like alligator skin."

"Look, there's a deer!" said Angela. A large deer was grazing nearby. Realizing it had been seen, it swished its white tail and bounded away.

Paul tugged his baseball cap to shade his face from the hot sun, and asked aloud, "If it's called the Lost Mine Trail, do you think there's really a hidden mine hidden here? Better look out, Ange, or you could fall into it," he smirked.

Just then, a hiker came down the trail, holding a long walking stick in one hand and a water bottle in the other. She smiled and looked at Paul. "If I heard correctly, you want to know if there's really a mine around here." Paul nodded, curious to hear what she knew about the mine but embarrassed that she had heard what he said to his sister.

"If you have a few minutes, I can tell you all about it," said the woman. She sat down on a large rock, took a drink from her water bottle, and began her tale. "It's an old legend that goes back to the days when Spain ruled this land. Nearly 500 years ago, Spanish explorers sailed to North America hoping to find gold and other riches. The legend tells that there was lots of gold in these mountains, and the Spaniards found it."

"The Spaniards claimed this land, built a strong fort and a prison near here, and called it *Presidio de San Vicente*, which means 'Saint Vincent's Fort.' They had come to this region with powerful weapons, and they used these weapons to capture many of the Native Americans who lived in the land around Big Bend. The Spaniards kept their prisoners locked up in the prison."

"Every day, the Spaniards forced their prisoners to hike up into the mountains and work in the gold mine. Each time the prisoners left the fort for the mine, the guards blindfolded them because the Spaniards did not want their prisoners to see where they were going. That way, they would never know how to get to the gold mine or tell its location."

"Mining was hard work to begin with, but the Spaniards would never let the prisoners take off their blindfolds," the woman continued.

"They had to work in blindfolds? How could they see what they were doing?" asked Angela.

The hiker nodded. "Most times they couldn't see, so they just did their best. But every now and then, some of the prisoners could peek beneath their blindfolds. They began to figure out the location of the mine and think about escaping. If they knew where the mine was, maybe they could come back one day and take some of the gold. But their cruel guards always watched them. They could not escape."

"One evening, no prisoners or guards returned to the Presidio. The Spaniards waited impatiently, yet no one came."

"The Spaniards were angry. Had their prisoners and guards stolen the gold? They decided to hunt down the prisoners and guards and make them very sorry."

"Then what happened?" asked Paul anxiously.

The hiker continued. "The angry Spaniards took their weapons and went into the mountains, but they lost their way. They hiked through the long, hot day and into the cold night, but they never found the gold mine, the guards, or the prisoners. In fact, they were so lost that they never found their way back to the Presidio."

"Years passed, but the Spaniards didn't return from the Chisos Mountains, and neither did their prisoners nor the guards. All anyone knows is that they all disappeared, and so did the gold mine and its riches. To this day, no one has found it, even though many people have tried."

"What are we waiting for? Let's find that mine and get some of that gold!" said Angela, with visions of dollar signs dancing through her head. "Are there any clues about where it might be?"

"Well," said the woman as she rubbed her chin thoughtfully, "The locals say that if you stand on the site of the old Presidio's doorway on a certain day in spring and look up into the mountains, the sun's first rays will shine on the hidden doorway to the mine."

"Isn't that amazing, Paul?" Angela sang, excitedly poking her brother in the chest.

"Who knows if the mine ever existed at all," shrugged the hiker, getting up to leave, adding, "I'm sure it's nothing but a legend." She said good-bye and headed down the trail, walking stick in hand. Seconds later, Paul and Angela were leading their parents back up the trail. All of them watched carefully for clues to the hidden gold mine as they hiked, dreaming of the fortune that might be buried somewhere deep in the mountains.

"Check it out!" exclaimed Paul a few minutes later, pointing to a small gap in the rocks far off the trail. "That looks like a hidden pathway to me!"

"Sorry to disappoint you, son," said Dad, taking a closer look. "But I think that's just a spot where rocks may have worn down."

Suddenly, Angela stopped and reached for a shiny rock by the side of the trail. "I found some gold! It must be from the Lost Mine!"

Mom smiled as she examined Angela's discovery. "Honey, that's just iron pyrite. Miners call it 'fool's gold.' I'm afraid you'll have to keep looking."

An afternoon full of false alarms left Angela and Paul disappointed. But Dad pointed out that while they never found the mine, they did hear a great story to share with their friends back home. As the Jordans finished their hike, the sun was setting, and Paul turned to take one last look up the trail. There, in the fading afternoon light, he saw something sparkling among the towering rocks.

"We'll come back to Big Bend soon," he said firmly, "because I'm going to find that Lost Mine!"

Check In What part of the Lost Mine legend do you think might be true? Why?

Where DINOSA Once Roam

Imagine a time when monsters roamed Earth. Picture gigantic crocodiles with enormous teeth, or huge dinosaurs with necks longer than five fifth-graders standing on each other's shoulders. If you think Big Bend looks like a place such creatures might have lived, you are right.

Big Bend's fossil record goes back 100 million years, before dinosaurs. It includes fossils of plants, fish, amphibians, reptiles, dinosaurs, and early mammals. These fossils can tell about prehistoric life and its **extinction**. When an animal or plant becomes extinct, it is no longer alive anywhere on Earth. By studying Big Bend's fossils, we can find clues to what life there was like long ago.

UBS

by Dennis Fertig

> Based on this diagram, how would you describe the size of a SuperCroc?

Modern Crocodile

Super-Croc

☐ = 1 ft.

THE SUPERCROC

More than 90 species of dinosaurs have been found at Big Bend, but one of the park's most famous finds is not a dinosaur at all. It is a dino-eating crocodile nicknamed SuperCroc. Its real name is Deinosuchus (DINE-oh-SUE-kuhs), which means "terrible crocodile."

SuperCroc was up to 50 feet long. Its large jaws were powerful enough to eat any dinosaurs that stepped too close to its watery home. How do we know SuperCroc was a dino-eater? Scientists have found lots of dinosaur bones in Big Bend covered with scars made by SuperCroc's six-inch teeth.

TURTLE VS. SUPERCROC?

Paleontologist Steve Wick's job is hunting for fossils in Big Bend, and it isn't easy. Temperatures there can reach 115 degrees, and off-road vehicles aren't allowed. Steve spends a lot of time hiking the hot desert in search of creatures from long ago.

During one hot hike in 2004, Steve noticed an area full of sharks' teeth and crocodile bones. A closer look showed dozens of thick shell pieces sticking out of a nearby hillside. Steve carefully **extracted**, or took out, the bits of shell and pieced them together like a prehistoric puzzle. They formed the top shell of an ancient turtle.

▼ Steve Wick (left) and another paleontologist dig out the fossil turtle shell.

The next morning, Steve returned with another paleontologist. They gently extracted the turtle's 140-pound bottom shell and carried it several miles through the desert to their truck.

Once the shell was safely back in the lab, Steve examined it and discovered a huge crack that was a wound that had healed before the turtle died. He also found tooth marks. Had this turtle escaped a SuperCroc attack? We'll never know. Still, the turtle was quite a discovery: a rare, newly discovered species, and yet another treasure from Big Bend.

Steve Wick's turtle wasn't the only recent discovery in Big Bend. In 1999, a group of paleontologists and college students were busy extracting the bones of some young, small dinosaurs in the park. While taking a break, student Dana Biasatti wandered away and found herself looking at more dinosaur bones. The bones were huge! Dana had found the neck bones of an adult Alamosaurus. Her discovery was the beginning of an exciting debate.

Read on

27

BIG BONES IN BIG BEND

The Alamosaurus Dana Biasatti had found in the rock was a **sauropod** that lived about 70 million years ago. Sauropods were dinosaurs that ate only plants. They had long necks and tails and very small heads, and they are the largest known dinosaurs.

The huge neck bones from Dana's dinosaur were really heavy. Some weighed nearly 1,000 pounds! Neck bones that big probably came from a dinosaur that weighed 50 tons and measured 100 feet long.

These Alamosaurus fossils were an important discovery, but they presented a tricky problem. What should be done with them? Paleontologists were excited to study them and wanted to move them to a lab. Museums hoped to display them. But there were others who wanted the bones to stay right where they were. They said the fossils were part of Big Bend and should not be removed.

The park decided to move the fossils to a museum, which led to another problem. Few vehicles were allowed in the park. How could they get something the size of these enormous Alamosaurus fossils out of Big Bend? The answer? Helicopters.

In 2001, the Alamosaurus bones were airlifted out of Big Bend and brought to the Dallas Museum of Natural History where they were cleaned and studied. Eventually, they inspired an exhibit at a new museum in Dallas called the Perot Museum of Nature and Science.

> Paleontologists had to extract and prepare the fossils carefully for their journey.

A BIG BEND DEBATE

The Alamosaurus bones sparked a debate about what to do with important fossils found in national parks. Should they be left where they are found, or should they be taken to museums and universities to be studied?

Leave them where they are.

Many people believe nothing, not even special fossils, should be removed from a national park. They argue that national parks exist to protect precious natural resources, including fossils, and scientists could be allowed to study the fossils right where they are found.

Some local businesspeople suggested that the bones could become tourist attractions if they were left in the park. The bones could bring lots of visitors and their money to the region around the park. They wanted to see an amazing exhibit built around the fossil site.

Remove them.

Paleontologists agreed that fossils should rarely be removed from a national park, but they argued that Alamosaurus and similar fossils are very important finds. They were concerned that keeping these fossils in place might allow erosion to destroy them over time.

They didn't want to build an exhibit around the bones. They argued that it would bring visitors into protected park areas. Some people might even try to damage or destroy the bones.

> Scientists use the fossils they find to build models of dinosaur skeletons. These models help them learn more about dinosaurs such as Alamosaurus.

Reach a solution. Everyone knew the bones were important and wanted to protect them in the best way possible. Those who wanted to keep the bones in Big Bend felt that the fossils could be safely studied right where they were found. Those who wanted to remove the bones believed that the best plan was for scientists to study and preserve them in museums or at universities.

The solution was a compromise between both views. The Alamosaurus went to a museum in Dallas. However, park officials are developing a Fossil Discovery Trail with a charitable group called Friends of Big Bend. The trail will highlight fossil finds that remain in the park. It will also support the local tourist economy. Yet the most amazing finds will remain off-site where scientists will study them.

Check In Do you think scientists should be allowed to take dinosaur bones from the park? Explain.

Discuss

1. What connections can you make among the four selections in this book? How do you think the selections are related?

2. Why was the Big Bend ecosystem named as a biosphere reserve? How does that help protect and preserve the different habitats within the park?

3. What can bird-watching teach you about the different habitats in Big Bend National Park?

4. How would you summarize the debate about taking dinosaur bones out of Big Bend? Was the solution a good one? Explain.

5. What do you still wonder about Big Bend National Park? How can you learn more?